BÔ YIN RÂ

(JOSEPH ANTON SCHNEIDERFRANKEN)

VOLUME SIXTEEN
OF THE 32-VOLUME CYCLE
THE GATED GARDEN

CEREMONIAL MAGIC AND MYTH

For information
about the books of Bô Yin Râ and
titles available in English translation
visit The Kober Press web site at
http://www.kober.com

THE KOBER PRESS PUBLISHES THE ONLY ENGLISH TRANSLATIONS
OF THE BOOKS OF BÔ YIN RÂ AUTHORIZED BY THE KOBER VERLAG,
SWITZERLAND. THE KOBER VERLAG PUBLISHES THE BOOKS OF
BÔ YIN RÂ IN THE ORIGINAL GERMAN AND HAS PROTECTED
THEIR INTEGRITY SINCE THE AUTHOR'S LIFETIME.

BÔ YIN RÂ
(JOSEPH ANTON SCHNEIDERFRANKEN)

CEREMONIAL MAGIC AND MYTH

TRANSLATED FROM THE GERMAN
BY JAN SCHYMURA, MALKA WEITMAN
AND ERIC STRAUSS

THE
KOBER
PRESS

BERKELEY, CALIFORNIA

This book is a translation from the German of *Kultmagie und Mythos* by Bô Yin Râ (J.A. Schneiderfranken), published in 1924 by Verlag Magische Blätter, Leipzig. The copyright to the German text is held by Kober Verlag AG, Bern, Switzerland.

Printed in the United States of America

International Standard Book Number: 978-0-915034-24-6

Typography and composition by Dickie Magidoff

Book cover after a design by Bô Yin Râ

CONTENTS

PREFACE

ONE SHOULD NOT EXPECT A SCHOLARLY treatise here.

What is presented here does not pretend to be a historical account.

Nor is it a contribution to the study of archeology.

The waters of living wellsprings flow freely here!

Life shall blossom from them.

Life and responsible action.

Understanding is to be imparted here, so that one may distinguish between sublime things and the human lust for power that, since time immemorial, has appropriated matters touching the sublime and used them to its own ends.

And finally, the never-changing, sacred path —the path that leads the wanderer to the Light—is shown from yet another vantage point.

❧

CHAPTER ONE

HUMANITY'S CREATIVE WORKS

I KNOW OF NOTHING GREATER ON THIS EARTH than the works humanity has created when inspired by the spirit within.

When human beings, awed by the magnitude of what they themselves are able to create, fashion gods in their own image—especially then do I admire their creations.

Even when they finally say: We realize now that those works we have revered and took to be the acts of gods, are in truth the works of mortal beings—the worth of those noble works is not diminished.

I know that all things spiritual need human beings in order to become manifest on this earth and perceptible to mortals in this life.

Indeed, I am able to honor even humanity's self-created gods for humanity's sake!

I see humanity's most noble qualities in these self-created gods.

I see humanity's greatness in the creations of the human mind, which human beings raised up above themselves and to which they now pay homage.

Human beings enthroned an image of their own majesty only to then bow down before it.

Thus many enlightened forms of worship and the profound myths that sustain them are sacred to me—for the sake of humanity, because they are the work of humanity.

In myth I see humanity in its divine form.

In their rituals, I see human beings worship the divine in themselves—named with the name of a god they themselves have created.

✤

TRULY, YOU must think very little of yourself if you feel justified in scorning these sublime works—humanity's gods, myths and forms of worship, which it has created for itself.

You still are a stranger unto yourself, if you look for signs of the Spirit on this earth, and yet disdain these forms of worship and these myths because they have been fashioned by mortals.

❧

THE SAGES of olden times knew in their wisdom that they must conceal from immature souls the knowledge that they themselves had created that which they proclaimed to be the words of the gods.

Also those who heard the voice of the God-head within themselves created gods who could carry its majesty and power—because this voice was too frightening for humans to bear on their own.

They described these gods through image and allegory—likenesses of the divine that seemed to them to be true reflections of the Godhead—and others who received their words in time brought forth new images and allegories.

However, those who understood the mysteries of the divine, sages who knew the far reaches of the spiritual power that mortals possess, created rituals that made use of myth—enlightened rites whose magical power, hidden behind allegory and image, summon the human being's most secret powers.

Much that was once humanity's treasured possession, held sacred for millennia, lies buried today.

Yet much still possesses its magic, hardly recognized today by those who take part in these rites.

&

THOSE WHO hold such worship in contempt, because they know that human beings were creators of the myths on which it rests, mistakenly believe that their discovery strips myth and worship of their worth, exposing them to be mere foolishness and delusion.

They do not realize that the wise person knows how to honor that which they choose to spurn.

They do not realize that they stride over the fundaments of temples, inside whose walls priceless treasures still wait to be found.

Instead they see the workings of mortals behind the creations they had attributed to gods—and now disdain as worthless that which once they had worshipped.

Few are those who can perceive within themselves the heights to which humanity's works may reach.

They alone still hold in awe the works created by human beings past.

They know that every great culture that has ever existed has been raised to noble heights by rituals sustained by the power of myth.

They understand that myth and sacred ritual cannot be created through the arbitrary will of any person. This is why they honor what human beings have brought forth from the depths of their creative power.

None have measured how deep go the depths of the wellspring from which this power flows.

When one searches the inner reaches of one's soul, and listens to its stirrings within, one will soon enough find that by despising the work of the sages, one is only slandering oneself.

Overcome with awe, one will then stand humbly before these works of mortal humans, in which the Godhead is revealed.

CHAPTER TWO

MYTH AND REALITY

S HROUDED IN THE DISTANT NIGHT OF TIME ARE the harrowing trials that had oppressed humanity in ages past and moved human beings to create the first dark myth.

❦

ONCE AT HOME in the glow of the fiery light of eternal love, the timeless human spirit— brought into existence to shine for all eternity —suddenly found itself a fallen star amidst the horrifying chaos of this earth.

Now merely a creature among creatures, the timeless spirit of the human being was not, however, abandoned completely by the light.

Unhappier than its fellow creatures, it became aware of an unspeakable loneliness; an aloneness it had once longed for and had created for itself before understanding what this would mean.

And now it was unable to endure that very thing it once had sought with such longing.

Endowed from the first with creativity, the fallen human spirit still possessed its creative spark. Even in its most profound godforsakenness, the earth-bound, creature self could not wrest this power away from the being's timeless essence.

It took refuge now in this creative power and, in the depths of its agony, created images to remind itself of the realm of light from whence it had come— images, albeit murky and confused, that were a reflection of the home it had once willingly fled.

❧

THE OVERWHELMING forces of nature, which helpless humans felt looming over them with menacing might, commanded a place in the myths that mortals created.

Nature's acts of destruction, those that showed no mercy to humanity, were thought to be the deeds of cruel demons, whose wrath the powerless could only appease through sacrificial offerings.

Nature's beneficent acts, those that brought peace to the tormented, fallen spirit, were thought to be the deeds of kindly and well-disposed gods, whose favor could only be courted through offerings of gratitude and praise.

&

OF THE MANY who shared in this earthly existence, each one added to the fabric of the original story, this image of a transcendent world, until no one was aware any longer that they themselves had woven the cloth of that which now formed their faith.

And so, the first myth was born and gained power over humanity! Countless variations have sprouted from this seed, scattered through the earth and transmitted from generation to generation.

For a long time, only the desperate need of the earth-bound human being was reflected in such myths.

&

Bᴜᴛ ᴛʜᴇɴ ᴄᴀᴍᴇ some who spoke of sublime wonders they had experienced in solitude and silence.

The hierarchies of the spiritual world had taken pity on the fallen human spirit lost within the creature self and wanted to show it the path back to its eternal home.

The way to salvation, however, could only be opened by human beings themselves. Thus, the spiritual helpers of humanity sought to find those few who could be prepared to become mediators of eternal Light—Luminaries who, through themselves, would bring light to others.

They were found in the heart of Asia, and from there they went forth through all the world, faithful to their calling.

Among each of the earth's peoples one of them suddenly appeared, and their words lit a holy flame in all who heard them. But what they said was too sublime for mortals to bear in its pure form.

And so the Luminaries' truth merged with the myths that were alive for the peoples of each time and place. In this way, those myths were lifted up, becoming in time image and likeness of the most sacred wisdom.

Thus, the most secret knowledge was transmitted to countless numbers.

☙

But there also were many whom the light could not reach, for their spirits had been shrouded in darkness by the dense, creature self.

And the light struggled with the darkness, but the darkness remained victorious.

The myth took on many new guises, and the light and life that had infused it once now hardened into petrified stone—the pillars of a temple of idols.

☙

The luminaries, born anew into each generation, came forth from their deepest seclusion, seeking to save that which could still be saved on this earth. But only the smallest few in each age could be found. Most continued to heedlessly stumble along the path of illusion, fettered ever more to the creature self and the demon of the earth, far removed from all longing for light.

The harrowing night of soul-extinction threatened to swallow all humanity. In this time of urgent need, the spiritual hierarchies took pity once again on fallen humanity, enslaved by the creature self. They sent forth a Luminary charged with a mission that no one before had been willing to fulfill—and having fulfilled it, none who came after could be asked to achieve.

Out of love beyond all understanding, he had offered himself up for this mission, even while still in the Spirit's realm.

In preparation for his task, he had refined his power of love to greatest purity while still dwelling in the Spirit's realm, before taking on his human form on earth.

As the greatest of Compassion's Mediators who ever walked this earth, he fulfilled through his death what he had undertaken to fulfill.

In his hour of death on Golgotha the invisible aura of the earth was transformed through him so that now, all who are determined to turn from darkness toward the light, all who seek earnestly, with fervent heart and soul—*must* be granted salvation. What the mightiest could barely achieve before his compassionate deed on Golgotha—was now within reach through him!

And even though this earth's darkness remained, it no longer had the power to fetter those mortals truly determined to resist it.

It's all-consuming might had been forever broken by this one human being's act of compassion.

છ

TO BE SURE, the greatest of Compassion's Mediators had infused with light the myth of his people and time.

To be sure, he had shown to all the sublime wisdom the myth of his time held within it, separating truth from delusion that threatened to extinguish its light.

To be sure, as the first among his Brothers, he transmitted clearly and purely the teachings of the Spirit that were his to give, without weaving them into myth, as teachers before him had thought fit to do.

⟨⟩

He could not, however, prevent what would come when his own time on earth was done: that others who followed would weave his own teachings into myth—and even the account of his life would itself become myth.

In this myth also, through imagery and allegory, eternal wisdom could be found.

In this myth also, truth was intertwined with error. One must sharply distinguish each from the other so that delusion will not strangle the truth. The last great myth humanity created must now be clarified to reflect the Reality that is at its source.

⟨⟩

Myth has served humanity for thousands of years, bringing light into the darkness of night. But now the time of teaching through myth is complete—the age of knowing directly has dawned!

Coming generations will truly know how to honor the myths of ages past. They will regard them, however, as images seen in a mirror: just as one may see an image of one's countenance, but not the face itself.

Over time, humanity will seek other ways to ignite the spark of its creative power. Even if actual events appear to support the validity of its myths, humanity will surely be able to distinguish between the ultimate Reality that lies at the ground of all being, and its reflection in allegory and image.

The power myth held once and still holds today over humanity's minds and hearts, wherever the faith it inspired still lives, will fade away in the era to come, never again to return.

The life of the Spirit, which myth could only mirror, will infuse human beings in these coming times, so that they themselves will be able to comprehend truths their ancestors could only approach through the mirror of myth.

Until that time, however, may the myths of the ancients be everywhere revered as humanity's spiritual creation.

❧

CHAPTER THREE

MYTH AND RITUAL

THOSE HUMAN BEINGS WHOSE FAITH WAS formed by myth needed always to honor the gods and to thank them, or to placate malevolent spirits.

The only way to do this, it seemed to them, was through action in the external world.

They came to believe that not just their action mattered, but also the form that it took.

Not every form of sacrificial offering, or giving thanks and praise, seemed to be favored equally by the gods.

Thus they ceased to practice forms of sacrifice and worship that did not appear to please the gods and practiced other forms that would, as they believed, win them the gods' favor.

To guarantee the fulfillment of their wishes, those practices that seemed to bring success were rigorously observed.

The rituals through which the gods were worshipped had now become fixed in form.

⚭

Human beings felt themselves duty bound to the heavenly beings that their own minds had created—until the first of the Luminaries appeared, to bring light unto the myth.

It was they who freed the worship of the gods from the fetters of dark superstition and used it instead to awaken humanity's magical power that lay dormant within.

They knew that human beings possessed the power to influence the invisible world and to summon its forces to serve their will.

They knew also that total inner confidence was needed for success. For this reason, they anchored human beings' magical endeavors to the firm foundation of whatever faith was most established at that time.

And so human beings came to believe that the energies they felt stirring within them, which came from themselves alone, instead were a gift of the gods, bestowed by their favor and grace.

Humanity had not matured enough—and still is not mature enough today—to test the limits of the sublime power that is theirs, and to bear the weight of knowing it is theirs alone.

❧

ALTHOUGH THEIR MAGIC did not produce immediate results, their prayers and pleas, it seemed, now were "heard" with greater certainty.

Because light had infused their myths, humanity's rituals had been lifted up to touch the divine, awakening the sound of the soul in the faithful and stirring its deepest resonances.

In later times, decay and petrification destroyed the life within the rituals, leaving only a sterile, outer shell.

And yet, a memory of an earlier, more blessed time remained, kept alive through legend.

❧

TETHERED TO THE struggle for survival, humanity dreamt of a magical world in which it could subdue the forces of nature with ease.

Legends arose in which the ancestors were endowed with super-human powers, and gods dwelt among humans on earth.

There were others who surmised that living rituals still were practiced in clandestine circles, where the legacy of ancient times was remembered and preserved.

Those who practiced in secret guarded the sacredness of what they had preserved, thus arousing the curiosity of others. Unscrupulous individuals took advantage of the air of mystery surrounding this legacy to endow themselves with false authority.

The duplicity of priests has its beginnings in those prehistoric days.

What history has recorded of these ancient rituals comes from a late stage in their existence.

Historians would need to recover thousands of years in the early history of these rituals, now lost to us, in order to establish their origins with certainty.

ॐ

BUT THOUGH SO much treasure lies buried, still a meager remnant remains—carried forward into historic times and preserved even until today. Not everything the ancients knew has vanished from the earth.

In Europe, a "new" faith preserves much of this precious inheritance today, with full awareness of the need to protect it from the touch of profane hands; in the heart of Asia a younger faith, similar for good reason to the one that flourished in Europe, also gives new form and interpretation to the heritage from times long past.

❧

IT WOULD BE FOOLISH today to found a new faith that would owe its strength to myth, like the ones I mention here.

It would be foolish above all to found a new faith based on a myth on which an already-existing faith rests.

Yet, who can prevent those who have left their faith, yet still believe the myths on which that faith was based, from returning to rituals in the form they were originally practiced, when antiquity first appropriated and adapted them to serve the then-new myth? Who can stop these believers if their need for worship based on venerated myth still lives within them?

The rituals created in the not too distant future will no longer be based on myth.

These new forms of worship will derive their power from the essence of ancient rites and will be purest ritual magic that calls upon the innermost powers human beings possess.

But these future practices cannot be created arbitrarily, simply out of longing for them.

The energies required for this to happen must first have been awakened and made active in many.

When this state has been reached, these practices will inevitably come into being, no matter what stands in their way.

The seed has been implanted in the womb of the invisible soil from which it will one day send forth sturdy shoots, and grow into a tree.

Its fruits will nourish a coming culture.

The longing of the many who want this to happen will awaken, more and more, the germinative power of the seed from which these new practices will grow.

❧

CHAPTER FOUR

RITUAL AS A
FORM OF MAGIC

H UMAN BEINGS CREATED CEREMONIES to worship the gods they had fashioned, believing that they must serve their gods in the
way they served their kings. But the Luminaries lifted up these rituals, infusing them with
light and imbuing them with magic.

At this time, however, only a select few were
allowed to learn the secret nature of these
rituals.

Most of humanity had not yet attained the
inner maturity—the wisdom of the soul—
needed to bear the full knowledge of their own
spiritual might without endangering their soul.

The human spirit remains so subjugated to
its animal nature, in this earth-bound realm
where it has taken refuge, that even today
most human beings would suffer harm to their

soul were they to comprehend the power they hold in invisible realms.

Ultimate truth, however, does not need to be hidden nowadays, because those who cannot receive it hide it from their own eyes, even when it appears in brightest sunlight and is made visible to all the world.

They are shielded from the truth through their own lack of faith.

Thus it is possible to speak of many things today that the sages of old had to hide from humanity in an age when faith was strong, a time when human beings were still connected closely with the invisible realm, and so needed to be protected from themselves.

Even in our day, only an elect few will come to understand the mysteries of their spiritual power, because they alone are able to comprehend its reach.

These elect few, however, are far more numerous today than at any time before.

Only they will be able to nourish their souls with my words and be inspired by them to awaken new experience.

∞

We are speaking here of sacred rites insofar as they call forth magic that can benefit the individual.

The Godhead needs human beings so that it may be known to mortals—but has no need of human praise or rituals performed on its behalf. Rituals exist to serve the human being; they have a magical effect that can awaken human souls from their slumber and release them from the snares of the creature self. Such rituals may open a new realm of possibility to individuals in which they are assured that spiritual help is always near, even when the creature self has met the limits of its power.

❦

The word "magic" has fallen into disrepute.

Charlatans in all ages have robbed it of its true meaning.

Yet magic is still present in every aspect of this life!

It is a curse for all who want to use it to satisfy their earthly, animal desires.

It becomes a blessing when infused with love.

This is why all high ritual magic is so powerful: because concealed within it, hidden beneath layers of veil, is the creative force of love.

❧

ONE MAY SPEAK OF ritual magic only when, during the ceremony, the many become as one—and such a union can come into being only through the power of love.

Here the mystery is revealed, when priests of a newer faith bless the congregation, intoning words preserved from fragments of the rituals of old:

"The Lord be with you!"

And when this blessing echoes back from the multitude:

"And also with you!"

❧

ALTHOUGH FOR MOST who join together in the community of such a faith, this blessing has been reduced to mere formula, it nevertheless indicates to us the conditions that must exist to release the magical potential within sacred ceremonies.

Here, in a form handed down from long ago, the energy of all those participating in the magic ritual is lovingly transmitted to the priest, who receives it, and a union of souls comes to pass.

Empowered by the enormous accumulation of the forces of participating souls, the priest, uniting within himself the will of all, commences and completes the supreme magical work.

The interpretation ordinarily given to this work is far removed from what the ritual actually brings into being.

That which is ardently wished for by those who are united in will, strong in faith and connected through love—a love that flows forth when one's deepest faith is shared with others —cannot be touched by any dogma.

The Godhead which, through the magic of ritual, is to be induced for moments to make itself felt within the human spirit as something having entered this world of earthly senses, is in truth very far removed from such magical observance. Nonetheless, at such moments, the faithful will indeed experience ultimate Reality.

☙

The ancient faith that here received new life deemed bread, the source of human beings' nourishment, and wine, the drink that lent them vigor and enlivened the senses, as those earthly substances most worthy to receive the Godhead, were it to magically unite with matter.

Human beings sought this sacred union but knew no other experience than that gathered through the filter of their earthly senses, which had never been penetrated. And so this experience, too, could only become theirs through their bodily senses.

How else should their god unite with them except through food and drink, since only in this way can the human body assimilate that which enters from without.

☙

IT IS NOT RELEVANT here to ask how it is that matter might be transformed by magic. Of significance is solely what takes place in the consciousness of the faithful who partake of the bread and wine, not as physical matter but as bearers of the Godhead—whatever name they might bestow upon the deity—in a form that can be comprehended by the senses.

Those who are conscious and capable of experience in the realms of the unseen world know that fervent believers who partake of such a ceremonial meal are not in any way deceived.

❧

IT IS NOT THE BREAD and wine that bring about, at moments of the highest concentration once bread and wine have been consumed, that vibratory change in the spiritual substance of the faithful. Rather, it is the magical force that springs from faith itself that makes it possible for them to sense the true and living spiritual energy of the divine.

Only a few have thus far known what this magical force can do when it flows in concert from many who share the same faith and intention.

This accumulated force flows back to all individuals who share that faith and intention, even to those who did not participate in its awakening during the ritual.

❧

THE MODERN FORM of worship that owes its heritage to this ancient one is truly built upon a firm foundation, despite the fact that many view it with disfavor, believing it to harbor only darkest superstition.

It is the dogma that the faithful have formulated out of the myths they hold sacred that leads to erroneous interpretations of the rituals based on those myths. This does not alter in the least the fact that forces here come into play, awakened through observance of the rituals, that otherwise slumber deeply within.

⚯

CEREMONIAL MAGIC awakens these slumbering forces. It is a magic of symbols and sounds: It demands that practitioners use their own bodies to form magic symbols, in accordance with a strictly determined rhythm and sequence. Likewise, it requires that particular sounds be repeated many times, in a sequence that is strictly determined.

The content of the prayers in which this sound-magic is concealed—and not all prayers included in a particular rite have this magical character—is of no importance for achieving the desired effect.

This use of sounds in a magical way is the reason why it is so important that the required words be spoken in the ancient language from which these rites originated. The power of these rites is diminished by half when this is not so.

Whether or not those who still practice these rites know what they are doing is irrelevant, just as is the interpretation they give them, or the reasons that newcomers may give for wanting to change them.

❧

CEREMONIAL MAGIC is not mere symbolism!

Ceremonial magic is based on strict laws, inherent in the structure of the spiritual world, that awaken magical forces that lie dormant within.

❧

VENERABLE INDEED is that remainder of an ancient ritual practice still preserved today —thousands of years older than people are willing to admit, even though they might suspect as much. Venerable too are the ritual practices preserved in the two-thousand year old faith to which my words primarily relate, as well as those of the younger faith still practiced in the heart of Asia.

In addition, many fragments of ancient magic ceremonies can be found among the peoples of the earth.

One often considers certain ritual practices to be primitive when, in fact, they are the withered fragments of enlightened rites derived from prehistoric times. Similarly, the peoples who perform these rites are not at the beginning but, rather, at the most inglorious end of a spiritual life that was at one time incomparably higher.

Highly developed cultures were forced into retreat as human beings increasingly succumbed to the lower instincts of the creature self, and enlightened forms of worship were replaced by sorcery and fetishism.

Whenever human beings indulge their creature self and, in so doing, surrender to the demon of the earth, only a caricature remains of the glory that enlightened cultures once created to bring human beings close to the divine.

❧

CHAPTER FIVE

MAGIC AND SPIRITUAL COGNITION

THE MAGICAL RITES OF THE ANCIENTS WERE created by sages who understood the laws that govern spiritual events.

Guided by the wisdom of the Spirit's light, they recognized that human beings must have both feet planted firmly on this earth before, with outstretched arms, they try to touch the heavens.

The sages were equally removed from both extremes into which so many humans fall: the lure of self-created ecstasy; the narrow and myopic earth-bound view that cannot see beyond the limits of one's immediate surroundings. Thus, they experienced within their inmost selves the sublime and incomparable union of all forces of the soul whereby the inner world expands to encompass everything external and everything external is experienced as the manifest expression of innermost events.

They knew how actions in the outer world could be shaped so as to reach the inmost self, and how to then employ those inner forces to transform the world outside.

By heeding the laws of the spiritual realm, they sought to release human beings and things of this world from earthly bondage.

They taught others how to use the forces of the external world to rouse the energies of inmost life—the only way to burst the bonds that cannot otherwise be loosened.

Enlightened magicians themselves, they taught the highest, sacred magic and thus became redeemers of their fellow humans, still fettered by the creature self.

They did not seek to transmit the kind of earthly knowledge that springs from mental thought, a type of understanding that may foster higher values but cannot ever lead to spiritual awakening.

They sought instead to foster *spiritual* cognition; a way of comprehending capable of unveiling things that cannot be revealed though mental thought—because these things are not found in this world of physical manifestation —the world of appearances—but exist only in the realm of ultimate Reality.

❦

ALL HUMAN THOUGHT is forever anchored in the world of appearances and the human mind, though it may imagine purely abstract matters, remains always of this world.

Just as one cannot jump over one's self even if one is the best of jumpers, in the same way, thinkers can never withdraw from the realm of thought—from the world of physical manifestation. And those who try, employing their razor-sharp thinking to do so, only turn themselves into fools without even noticing it.

Everything belonging to this world of appearances is that "outer" something that corresponds to something within. As such, it can never be grasped through thinking; because all thought, no matter to what heights it may rise, remains a function of the world of appearances, and is enclosed and bound by it, even if the object of thought itself may lie far beyond this earthly world.

Only a hazy reflection of the object can serve as the focus of thought. The object itself remains as it was and can never be clearly defined through means that are part of the world of appearances.

Ultimate Reality cannot be grasped through thought.

℘

THINKERS SUBSTITUTE thought for Reality. But all thought originates in the world of physical manifestation and can never escape its confines.

Spiritual worlds, too, are realms of manifestation, albeit of a more sublime nature than the worlds of manifestation of the material cosmos.

Even in these spiritual realms thoughts can never reach the innermost core—the ultimate Reality inherent in these worlds.

To be sure, thinking that occurs within the realms of Spirit is solely a function of spiritual organs and thus free of many hindrances by which the physical brain is bound. Still, these spiritual organs are a part of the worlds of spiritual manifestation and whatever may be perceived through them remains enclosed within those worlds.

Ultimate Reality can only be perceived with certainty when it reveals itself through inner experience.

Ultimate Reality can only be grasped through inner experience.

∞

THIS EXPERIENCE STANDS above all thought in its power and beyond all thought in its nature.

To bring about such an experience, the enlightened masters of a time before recorded history taught the pure, unsullied magic that they embedded within rituals.

In this way the purest ceremonial magic was passed on—the last remains of which can still be found on earth.

∞

ARCHEOLOGISTS HAVE unearthed the foundations of ancient temples in which these rites were once performed.

There they found many ritual implements and fragments illustrating teachings from prehistoric times. However, the holiest mystery of these sects perished along with their celebrants who, in those distant days, thought it to be a gift of the gods and protected it from profane influences. So completely did they guard this mystery that even the most intensive investigation will not yield insights as to its true nature.

Only those last remnants of these rituals that have been preserved in the language of ancient Rome as well as in the heart of Asia might reveal some insights here.

Yet even here the golden thread that shows the way to exit from the labyrinth can all too easily be lost.

Those who would hold fast to the golden thread will have to clearly recognize that ceremonial magic cannot be transmitted through the intellect but, rather, can only be reached through the highest innermost experience.

Only through such experience may human beings attain a kind of knowledge that cannot be shaken or destroyed, even by death of the physical body.

Only this knowledge is truly worth striving for!

❦

To those who have attained this knowledge, every world of manifestation—be it this world of the material cosmos or one of the worlds of spiritual substance—is now experienced as an expression and clear image of ultimate Reality.

Such individuals will comprehend each of these manifestations through their innermost Being, whether it be this life on earth or the manifold forms of life that the human spirit will experience when it sheds its mortal, physical body.

❦

Fables from days of old, arising as they do from a time of greatest human need, would have human beings believe that, after departing this earth, they will find themselves at once, with greatest clarity of being, in spheres of spiritual light.

Human beings would do well to disregard such deluded ideas, born of wishful thinking.

Whatever humans have not attained in this short span of time on earth will remain their task after departing this material realm— though that same inner awakening might have been attained before they left this earth.

No one will be granted what they have not earned, no matter in which sphere they may find themselves, because eternal laws are immutable and cannot be circumvented.

❧

HUMAN SPIRITS MAY dwell joyously in spiritual worlds for thousands of years, only to be seized by the same dread that grips them here on earth when they sense, at inspired moments, that beyond each lofty stirring of the soul there remains an even higher innermost that cannot yet be reached.

They then will need to seek the guiding hands of enlightened helpers—in the same way there as here—if they would be led into the innermost heart of Being.

First, however, they must prepare themselves so that they may be ready to receive this experience.

Once it has come to pass they will, to be sure, remain in the same spiritual realm of manifestation, but now as beings who have gained *real* knowledge and whom nothing can deceive. Similarly, should this experience come to pass while still on earth, they will not leave the physical realm.

⁊

CONTRARY TO THOSE fables that promise an effortless sojourn in spiritual realms after shedding the physical body, I must tell you that the task of reaching the ultimate, inescapable goal is much more difficult for those who have already shed their physical body. Indeed, human spirits who master the forces of their material nature while still in their mortal body are far more easily able to achieve the inner experience that alone leads to comprehension of ultimate Reality.

⁊

THE LUMINARIES OF eternal Light, who had lifted up the worship of the gods so that it became true ritual magic, understood the forces of this earth—the energies that seeking human spirits can learn to harness on their path.

This is why they joined the earth to heaven. This is why they created sacred rites that make use of earthly forces—symbols, sounds and tones—to reach the innermost, the deepest place in human beings wherein the holiest experience of ultimate Reality can be known.

❧

TRULY, HUMAN BEINGS nowadays should lament the fact that the path of ritual worship has been buried for thousands of years. Without its helping presence, one is left to submit to baseless and convoluted dogmas, the products of human arrogance.

And yet the path to true experience is not in any way closed.

A different path has been prepared that leads beyond the debris of ruined temples and into the holy land within the innermost soul.

I have described this path in many of my teachings.

I have set milestones for all who wish to find it.

Those who have embarked on this path feel themselves drawing ever closer to the goal; others have already reached it.

They do not miss the ancient temples where enlightened rituals were practiced nor the inner help that ritual magic offered. Because they are imbued with knowledge of the Spirit gleaned through inner experience, they are, however, able to recognize the traces of the Living Spirit that remain in many of these temples, and to give due honor to the magic of the ancient rites.

၈

THE PATH THAT LEADS into the heart of one's innermost and that is open to all throughout time is different for each individual even while it remains the same for everyone.

All will find their own way, according to their own distinct nature, on the same path that others are walking as well.

Only upon having reached their goal will seekers realize that they have been on that same journey together, and although each person's travels were different, none was easier or more difficult than another.

All who walk upon this path will stride from insight to insight until, having reached their goal at last, they come to know their own true self, and in their self behold the sanctuary wherein the Godhead reveals itself as their own Living God.

CHAPTER SIX

THE INNER LIGHT

L OST IN THE DARKNESS OF THE CREATURE self, the human spirit dimly perceived its true nature and the fate in which it was trapped, and projected its story outward as myth.

Very faint indeed was the ray of inner light that still remained, yet it allowed human beings to discover the first steps along the path that leads the spirit home, freed from the bonds of the mortal, creature self and returning to itself.

The few who recognized this path were able in the earliest of times, long before history was written, to reach the living Light within—the light within the human spirit that cannot ever be completely extinguished. By groping blindly and following the wisdom of their intuition, they reached the sacred goal and experienced the Living God within themselves—although they could not know its proper meaning.

But it is not the interpretation one gives to this experience that determines its value; rather, it is the reality of the experience itself!

Those who had not experienced this light within themselves looked instead to the lights of the outer world—the illumination of mental knowledge—which are kindled by the energies of the creature self. Now all their efforts were directed towards keeping this worldly light burning, fueling its flame through the flow of mental thought—just as oil might be poured on the wick of a lamp. Dazzled by the brightness of the blaze they had lit, most were distracted from their yearning for the light within—the only light that alone can illuminate the path to the Spirit.

For most human beings even the knowledge that such inner light existed was lost; and many who remembered it no longer paid it heed, so blinded were they by the glare of the light that they themselves created to illumine the external world.

In the darkness that engulfed them, the light of this world appeared to shine ever more brightly, and soon they could no longer even imagine they might have need of illumination of a different kind.

⚛

Even today many are enthralled by the light of this world and to them it seems the sum and substance of light.

Yet the soul remains in darkness, despite all the glitter of this worldly light, and its anxious calls cannot forever be ignored.

Thus many individuals feel the incompleteness, at some time in their lives, of their self-created light, and question the assumption that it holds all truth and fills every human need. They search on often curious paths to find the inner light—the light the ancients spoke of, the light they heard of from those who found it in themselves.

They examine many ancient myths for guidance as to how to reach the inner light and for traces of the secrets that the ancient rituals held.

⚛

THE MYTHS AND remnants of ancient rites that are still alive today contain many teachings as to how one may arrive at an experience of this inner light. However, most seekers are bound to the external world and are merely searching for answers from without, guided by the light that thought has created.

Thus, their seeking leads only to the knowledge of external things, and does not reach the inner self, and the interpretations given to this knowledge only take them farther from the truth.

༄

ONE MUST KNOW how to regard myths as the sages intended: as the image and reflection of an inner and innermost experience. Only then can these myths clearly point seekers in the right direction, as they set upon their path.

Each last remnant of ritual magic that has been preserved, or whose traces can still be recognized through the accounts in ancient writings, can serve to open the eyes of one who earnestly seeks to attain the inner light anew.

༄

IN ALL CEREMONIAL magic, outer and inner worlds are united, and it is through the outer world that the innermost is reached.

Nothing in the outer world exists for its own sake alone!

Because of their beauty, their effect on the senses, and expressive power of the symbols they contain, one might assume that ritual practices are complete in themselves. In truth, however, ritual is but a means to reach the soul of the seekers, so that they may know their true being, the innermost that waits to be awakened within.

❧

HERE IN THESE rituals, the remnants of ancient, sacred wisdom is revealed and may still serve humanity today.

It is essential to understand that everything external is connected to the human being's innermost self. And so long as one's endeavors to comprehend the things of this world are illuminated only from without—through the light of mental knowledge—they can only be known in a fragmented way.

It is essential to understand that every event in the external world affects the world within.

It is essential to understand that every activity in daily life can be lifted to the level of ritual magic, and used to awaken the inner life, if one approaches each activity with this pure intention.

❧

As yet, only a few are conscious of the responsibility they bear for every thought they think, however imperceptible, every word they speak and every deed they do in this external world.

Most do not know—and many do not wish to know—that words and thoughts affect the inner world of human beings in just the same way as deeds that have been done, and that through their thoughts, words and deeds they form their own inner world in a beneficial or deleterious way and influence as well the inner world of others as either blessing or curse.

❧

All those who read these words must ask themselves if they are willing, from this time onwards, to consciously shape the words, thoughts and deeds they put forth into the world in such a way that they become a blessing for themselves, for all those who live with them and for all those who will come after them on this earth.

Only those who are so willing can create the conditions that eternal law demands, and that they alone can bring about, if the inner light is to reveal itself to them.

❧

Many hold the vain belief that they must do "great things" in this external world in order to benefit themselves and others. But this kind of thinking is almost always a delusion, and things they think will be a benefit will often bring disaster.

They focus their attention on such outward actions, which are visible to all, yet they are very far from disciplining their thoughts or words or deeds when they believe that these are hidden from the world.

Thus many feel the call to bring happiness to entire peoples, while they themselves are still enslaved to their own thoughts.

❧

TRULY, THOSE WHO still deceive themselves in such a way may not expect to find the inner light within.

Those who would attain this light must attend their daily tasks—be they visible to many or hidden from the public gaze—in a conscientious manner. They must not succumb to the delusion that the only deeds that matter are those that history will record.

And if their life's path should lead them to positions of responsibility for many, then they must be all the more careful not to regard their mundane, daily obligations as unimportant, even if they are hidden and unrecognized by others in the outside world.

∞

THE ABILITY TO INFLUENCE invisible forces through action in the outer world—which the magic of the ancient rituals could only achieve during the celebration itself—will become for seekers who have embarked on the high path of liberation that I show them the means by which they may sanctify each moment of their earthly lives.

They will come to understand that all their thoughts, words, and deeds are instruments for working magic, insofar as every action in the physical dimension of this earthly life impacts also the invisible realm.

In this way seekers will bring about their soul's awakening and sense within themselves—depending on the ardor of their striving—that help from the Spirit is always near. Whereas before, they barely knew of matters spiritual and, had anyone spoken to them of these things, they would have felt such help to be beyond all possibility and would have dismissed such talk as fairy tales.

Through this help from the Spirit, seekers will know themselves to be securely guided on their path, until their soul is prepared to experience the inner light at last.

Immersed in this inner light, they will find themselves safe for all eternity and every final question about the meaning of human existence will be answered through their own experience, in a way that leaves no doubt.

❧

CHAPTER SEVEN

CONCLUSIONS ONE SHOULD DRAW

HUMAN SPIRITS WHO HAVE LOST THEMSELVES in the unruly, demanding animal of the earth nevertheless remain connected to their original home in the Spirit's realm, even if they are not conscious of it.

In the midst of their deepest darkness, a fleeting ray of light will at times stream faintly through—that very light they once had willfully turned away from. Though it may last for but a moment, it will evoke for them a memory, as of dreams dreamt long ago, in which human beings sense that they are something other than this mortal creature to which they feel so bound, which they have mistaken for their eternal self and upon which they have bestowed their own eternal name.

Such fleeting moments are the seed from which the human being's urge to find itself anew is born.

❧

ACCUSTOMED AS THEY are to trusting only in the energies of this material plane, human beings embark upon the inward search for self in the same way that they seek to fathom earthly matters.

Having set out in the wrong direction, they then inevitably conclude that all their seeking has been in vain—and this way of seeking only intensifies the darkness that surrounds them.

Without help from their primordial home in the Spirit—the only help that can here be of use—offered through high helpers who have been delegated to this task, lost human beings would be left to despair of ever finding their eternal self once again, while still on this material plane, or of overcoming the demon of this earth—"the Lord of Darkness."

❧

THE SOFT AND GENTLE rays of the Light of the Beginning may touch human beings from time to time, and may awaken a deeper longing for the Light—but the bonds with which the creature self has bound the human spirit cannot yet be loosened.

Human beings are not yet conscious of the vastness of their spirit, nor of its heights and depths, because what they regard as consciousness of their spiritual nature is in reality a state of mental awareness consisting of thoughts about their experience of life on earth.

In this earthly life, human beings are bound by many limitations and so everything that is not similarly bound they experience as being outside of and above themselves. Thus they have created a god—or gods—to act as vessels for those energies that cannot—or so it seems to them—be united with their constricted, creature self and which they cannot yet recognize as the essence of their own eternal being.

Thus also they created myths without suspecting for a moment that these myths are in fact stories of their own existence.

They then created forms of worship based upon these myths wherein the animal of the earth might have at last been forced to give way to their spiritual nature—yet they were unaware that here again the mortal creature had merely found a subterfuge in which to preserve its dominance.

❧

IF HUMAN BEINGS were to recognize who in truth they are, the animal would lose its hold and the demon of the earth its power. Instead, they set apart the best and highest in themselves and place it outside and above, and in so doing come to feel all the more the servant of the creature self and the cosmic despot that rules over it.

The Luminaries of eternal Light, who once infused rituals with spiritual power and lifted them to ritual magic, sought to free their erring fellow humans from the creature's powerful grip—but so tightly are human spirits bound that they cannot free themselves completely.

As he walked upon the earth, the greatest of Compassion's Mediators taught in clearest words that human beings have been given all the power they need to master the animal and the demonic forces of this plane—and to reclaim for themselves the glory they had conferred upon their gods. Yet his words were misinterpreted, so that human beings came to view the animal aspect of their nature as an enemy—that one may therefore torment but can never completely overcome.

Any impulse to unite the energies of the animal with one's eternal self was smothered by this misunderstanding. And with it also died all resolve to use the animal to serve humanity, in the same way one might use a beast of burden, which one would keep well nourished and in robust health, yet reined in so securely that it might be led to serve its master.

☙

TALES RECOUNTING THE sublime master's days on earth soon spread and became the basis for a new myth, and new rituals were in turn created from remnants of the old. And the clear and light-filled words uttered by the master were interpreted according to the confused and murky understandings of the people.

And yet, those practices that came into being in this way still have significance today, because in them are preserved the remains of ancient ritual magic that would otherwise have been lost.

Countless individuals are still connected to-day to their spiritual selves only through these remnants of ancient ritual magic, and spiritual help is able to reach them—even if the true source of such help is hidden from their eyes by the veils, richly decorated with wondrous stories and imagery, which the mythos of their faith has woven around ultimate reality, in arabesque-like and intertwined ways.

My words are not meant for those who are content with such a faith.

Nevertheless, they must endeavor to preserve what they possess and may rest assured that the path laid out by the teachings of their faith, though it may lead them into detours and through many dark terrains will, in the end—after they have passed through realms of imagery and story—allow them to reach their highest goal, so long as on this path they strive with fervent heart and soul to reach the realm of Spirit.

My words are meant for others.

My words are meant for those who ritual magic can no longer reach because they have outgrown the interpretations that tradition gives to those rituals, even if they still sense something, like the distant tolling of bells, that sounds from the liturgies of these rituals—a last testament to generations long gone.

॰॰

THE PATH THAT I AM called upon to describe allows those seekers who place their trust in it to reach the land of Reality, without having their view restricted by the walls that faith born of fear built for timid and anxious hearts.

All those who enter onto this path will find within themselves sure guidance, so long as they make themselves worthy of it through a transformation of will that unifies all of their soul forces and aligns them with a steadfast striving towards the highest goal.

But those who enter on this path in the same way that they fruitlessly explored so many other paths before—for the sake of curiosity or to increase their worldly knowledge— will soon find themselves alone and lost, with no sight of the trail.

Equally, this pure, high path will not welcome the footsteps of those who have not yet succeeded in taming their animal nature, however much they may wish to concentrate their soul forces to serve all things sublime.

No pact is possible here with the animal's insatiable drives and the consequences of actions taken while enslaved to the animal's nature can never be expunged.

❧

THE ANIMAL IN HUMAN nature will always have a thousand valid reasons to justify itself. Its beguiling voice will flatter human beings and convince them of the reasons that their instinctual drives should be followed and that their earthly needs will suffer deprivation if they pursue their soul's striving towards the Spirit.

The animal will attempt with every sort of cunning to preserve its power, enduring even contempt of itself and its desires—so long as human beings ultimately yield.

❧

THOSE WHO DO NOT wish to see the path that is supposed to lead them to self-knowledge become instead a road to their destruction must take care not to trust the animal's alluring voice.

They should, instead, speak kindly to the animal within them, saying: You, my creature self that is part of me, I am thankful for your strength. But know that from now on, your strength will be under my command! You will be transformed so that you now obey my will and serve me as your master!

❧

SUCH WORDS ARE LIKE a thunderbolt delivered to the animal—a shock that causes it to die. Yet just as the creeping caterpillar dissolves itself and dies so that it may emerge from its cocoon, transformed into a colorful butterfly, so too, the animal dies only to live again, transformed into a new way of being, purified and illuminated from within.

Those who had been slaves of their animal nature now become its masters, and the animal now willingly serves *them*, with renewed, sublimely transformed power.

This death and resurrection take place in the very same body, yet all the atoms of this body have now been spiritually renewed.

❧

THOSE WHO ARE ABLE to transform the animal within them will no longer be hindered by the demands of its existence.

It will become at one with the life of the Spirit.

Just as the body of the lute provides the chamber in which the plucked string's resonance can sound, so too will human beings' mortal bodies serve as the vessels within which their spiritual powers will unfold.

From this time on the Spirit alone will exercise all power.

The animal's own will, which had been the Spirit's enemy and constant adversary, is now extinguished.

❧

NOW AT LAST THE danger has been overcome that threatens all seekers who dare ascend to the heights before the animal in them has died and been resurrected, sublimely transformed and now in holy service to the Spirit's will.

❧

TO BE SURE, THERE have always been individuals who, conscious of their spiritual nature, rose to high levels of inner development without fully mastering their animal nature. However, one should not allow oneself to be fooled by those among them who achieved earthly fame.

None of these individuals had reached their highest goal while here on earth. None of them had experienced their Living God within, during their lifetime.

To be sure their spirit may have manifested itself in magnificent, lofty words, yet they remained disunited in themselves throughout their time on earth.

⁂

THOSE WHO ARE ABLE to absorb the wise words of such individuals will benefit from the profound spiritual value they impart. But if these seekers wish to attain full consciousness of their highest state of being in the Spirit's realm, they should not emulate the lives of these notables.

Many people who have lived their lives in obscurity and whose name no one has ever heard have achieved within themselves something indescribably higher than even the greatest of those who were able to climb to spiritual heights, but had not freed themselves from the fetters of the mortal creature.

ॐ

ONLY WHEN THE ANIMAL has been transformed and is completely united with the Spirit will the Mysteries not simply be intuited but, rather, fully *lived* and experienced with clear and awakened consciousness.

This experience can be opened for *every* soul.

For such a state to be experienced it is not necessary to believe in any myth nor is there need for any ritual that has its roots in myth.

In their highest form, rituals become raised up to ritual magic. So it is that one may say that the everyday life of human beings only becomes worth living and honorable from the moment human beings realize that all their actions have magical consequences—whether they are aware of them or not. The highest form of life is attained only when every thought, every word and every deed is purposefully taken and guided by the knowledge of their effect on the invisible dimension of physical events, as well as the knowledge of the effect of every impulse on one's own spiritual substance.

❧

HERE ON THIS earth, everything within is reached from without!

Human beings are only able to form their inner being by proceeding from the outside so that it may then be prepared to perceive the very innermost within itself.

Nothing in the external world can be considered too insignificant here!

❧

HAVING BECOME strangers to their original home in the Spirit, human spirits now find confirmation for their existence only through their thoughts, words and deeds in the external world—and only by proceeding from there are they able to return to themselves.

Everything in the external world must serve as a means to reach the inner life once again. Only in this way can human beings make proper use of the external world—the world of which their very bodies are a part.

❧

IN THESE MATERIALISTIC times there is a call for a new myth—but what is meant is a new form of worship.

And yet, a new way of worship to benefit all humanity will not emerge on earth until magic in its highest and most sacred form illuminates all life on earth.

Human beings' experience of the spiritual reality of their existence will then take the place of myth and from life itself the coming ritual magic will arise.

❧

For a deeper understanding
of the core of Bô Yin Râ's teachings
you may want to read:

The Book on the Living God,
The Book on Life Beyond and
The Book on Human Nature

These three books should be
read together.

A description of all three books follows.

The Book on the Living God

The Book on the Living God describes the inner path that leads to birth of the Living God within—what we must do and what to avoid on the long journey towards awakening the consciousness of our timeless self.

Ordinary consciousness, Bô Yin Râ tells us, is actually like sleep; there is a greater consciousness that is alive in us, informing every cell, and our task is to unite it with our self-awareness. Bô Yin Râ recommends practices to help us on the path: He counsels us to set aside time for daily contemplation and to meditate on words that touch and uplift us. Words in particular can be a gateway to an expanded sense of existence, because they embody hidden energies. The key is to experience their aliveness and not just understand them mentally. We should strive to master and unify the many thoughts and wills that struggle within us and cultivate attitude of quiet joy and serene detachment.

We must also set aside the ideas we have been taught about an anthropomorphic God. God is not meant to be an external object of worship but, rather, an experience to be awakened within us. We are cautioned to avoid the pitfalls that might divert us: following false teachers or believing that certain foods or exercises, or ecstatic experiences, have spiritual merit. Everyday life, when lived with attention to the ultimate goal, will lead us towards a gradual awakening of our timeless self.

E.W.S. Publisher

Contents: Word of Guidance. "The Tabernacle of God is with Men." The White Lodge. Meta-Physical Experiences.

The Book on Life Beyond

The Book on Life Beyond is a guide to help readers understand what they can expect to find in the life beyond death, and how to best prepare for it.

Bô Yin Râ explains that life beyond is actually another dimension of the same life we know here on earth—just as real and solid, but perceived through spiritual, rather than our limited, physical senses. He emphasizes the direct connection between our actions here on earth and their effects on life beyond. We bring with us into life beyond the same state of inner being with which we departed, and are able to experience its wonders exactly to the degree to which we have developed our spiritual self. For example, those who have failed to show compassion for others and have lived selfishly will find that life beyond lacks the warmth and light that other, more developed souls can perceive.

Bô Yin Râ counsels us to mentally practice the "art of dying" as a meditative practice to prepare for the transition from physical to spiritual existence. The goal is to constantly orient one's thinking, emotions and desires toward transformation of the self, in order to be able to receive the spiritual help that will be available to us after death.

E.W.S. Publisher

Contents: Introduction. The Art of Dying. The Temple of Eternity and the World of Spirit. The Only Absolute Reality. What Should One Do?

The Book on Human Nature

The Book on Human Nature presents basic concepts about human nature with the goal of inspiring readers to awaken the timeless, spiritual spark within. We become fully human only when the spiritual potential within us gradually awakens and infuses our material, purely animal selves. It is a path that every human being may and should pursue.

A central understanding is that all life results from the joining of opposites, in particular, the polarity of male and female energies. Bô Yin Râ emphasizes that the true spiritual human being is male and female united in one entity; when we seek our spiritual self, we must call forth the male and female in ourselves and in all things. He discusses the biblical fall from grace as a descent from the spiritual plane, in which male and female were united, onto a material plane, in which male and female are split apart.

Bô Yin Râ warns men that holding onto the illusion of male superiority means forfeiting their spiritual life. While the spiritual paths that are natural for men and women are different in tone—open and receptive for women, active and grasping for men—they are equal and complementary. He tells us that *true* marriage is preparation for the life beyond: by coordinating the desires, wills and attitudes of two beings we once again bring about, in some measure, the original state in which male and female energies are united.

E.W.S. Publisher

Contents: Introduction. The Mystery Enshrouding Male and Female. The Path of the Female. The Path of the Male. Marriage. Children. The Human Being of the Age to Come. Epilogue. A Final Word.